Time for MORE TEA

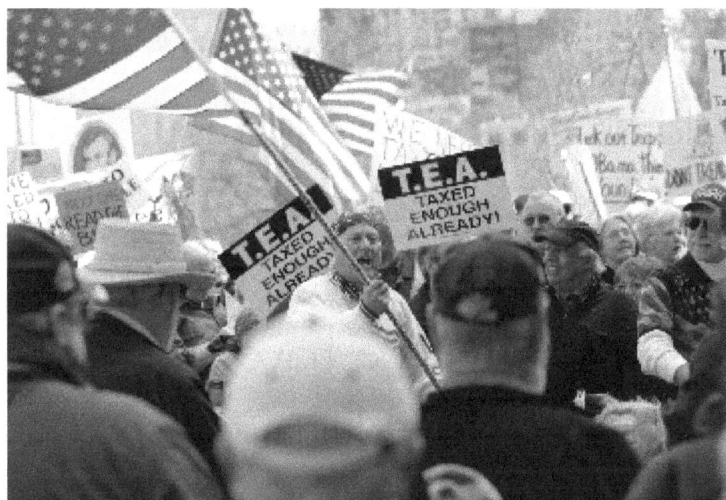

Wake Up AMERICA

We are the only country where we have homeless without shelter, children going to bed without eating, elderly going without needed meds, and mentally ill without treatment - yet we have a benefit for the people of Haiti on 12 TV stations, ships and planes lining up with food, water, tents, clothes, bedding, doctors and medical supplies. Imagine if we gave ourselves the same support that we give other countries. I feel bad for them, but I wonder who cares about America?

Time for MORE TEA

The Life saving way

Ron Berger

**The Life saving effects of drinking TEA
are gained
drinking it straight**

Published by:

berger publishing

Rancho Belago, CA 92555
Email - mail@ronberger.com
Web Page - www.ronberger.com

berger publishing

Printed in the USA
ISBN 13 - 978-0-9799257-3-3
ISBN 10 - 0-9799257-3-8
Volume II
First printing
Library of Congress Control Number: 2010921741

Time for MORE TEA

Ron's other books -

The House That Ron Built
(1-4137-8605-7) (978-1-4137-8605-7)
PublishAmerica, LLC

Are You Being Served Yet?
(1-4241-2485-9) (978-14241-2485-5)
PublishAmerica, LLC

P-NUT, The Love of a Dog
(1-59824-303-9) (978-1-59824-303-1)
E-Book Time, LLC

"Normal" MAYDAY
(0-9799257-0-3) (978-0-9799257-0-2)
berger publishing

Time for TEA
(0-9799257-1-1) (978-0-9799257-1-9)
berger publishing

Growing Old is a FULL-TIME JOB
(0-9799257-2-X) (978-0-9799257-2-6)
berger publishing

Author's Note:

E-mail messages and article clips used in this book are started with (**) and ended with (****) with credit given if the author and/or source is known.

I beseech everyone, who reads this book, to get involved and to lend their voice in turning this country around. I am not a member of the "radical right" or the "right wing conspiracy" but after reading this you will find that the "radical left" and the "left wing conspiracy" is growing fast.

Please also read the books by <u>Sarah Palin</u> and <u>Glenn Beck</u>.

Join the TEA PARTY while it is still possible.

Contents

ABOUT THE AUTHOR

Coming from a small town in Wisconsin, I was never exposed to much in the political realm. My dad was a Democrat, mainly because he was a union worker for the Electric Company, and he only looked for his benefits. My mother was a Republican (I think). Only one election did I get involved enough to actually offer my voting advise. It was 1948 when I heard Harry Truman talk and it made much more sense to me than Thomas Dewey that I advised my mother to vote for Truman. I don't know if she ever did, but Mr Truman was the last Democrat that made sense to me.

The election of 1952 was a no-brainer as far as I was concerned. I really felt sorry for Adlai Stevenson - and then for him to campaign against General

Eisenhower twice in four years was too much. Even the Democratic party tried to get Ike to run on their ticket in 1951. He was my Commander-in-Chief while I was in the USAF and I was proud of that fact.

My political life started to take shape when I was hired by a builder in California. That family was 100% Republican and you had better be also if you wanted to work for them. I didn't have to make any adjustment in my thinking and was on board with them from the first day. Nixon was our man and Kennedy was not. The next election in 1964 was Goldwater and not Johnson. We all know how those elections turned out.

During most Local, State and Federal elections I would automatically vote Republican. That doesn't mean that I thought they were better, but rather it was just easier. During the election of 1992 I broke that pattern and voted for Ross Perot. After he fell flat on his butt, I stopped voting altogether. I really couldn't tell the good from the bad. Oh, I had feelings, but figured that my vote didn't count anyway so why go through the hassle?

The last election between Obama and McCain really got me worked up. Not only did I feel this country now was going down the wrong path, but I felt an urgency about doing something about it. That's what most people felt, but didn't know what they should do about it. After about a year of receiving Obama bashing emails I realized that there has to be some truth to it. Then came the "Tea Party Brigades". I have never seen the general public so worked up and so wanting to turn this country around and take the control back from the Obama administration.

Now that a year has gone by with B. O. (Barack Obama) in charge, the meaning of "change" has really sunk in. He claimed that the USA was the best country in the world and he wanted to "change" it from the last administration. We now know that his change means socialism.

Lord, save us from those that think they know more than our founding fathers on how to run this country. This is the time for a complete change in Washington, DC. This is TEA TIME!

INTRODUCTION

I have read several books recently and have started several others. One book by Lee Iacocca *"Where Have all the Leaders Gone?"* is a shotgun approach to the Bush administration for all the stupid things that happened in eight years. I'm sure if he had waited several years to write his book, he would be focussing on the B.O. administration with much more meat to chew on. Bush had his shortcomings, but I truly believe he made a better president than Gore could have.

The next book is, *"Arguing with Idiots"* by Glenn Beck. One thing this book points out is that there are a great number of idiots in government. Glenn is not afraid to call a spade a spade and is not afraid to dig into many programs that the government has failed at completely and still pours money in to keep them afloat. This is a must reading for every conservative to understand just how incapable the federal government is at managing programs that they have no business getting into in the first place. If you don't feel sick to your stomach, then you didn't pay attention.

One of the best written and easily read books is *"Going Rogue"* by Sarah Palin. She is without a doubt, in my estimation, throughly qualified to run for president. Not only does she have much more experience than the present president, she can prove she is a "natural born citizen". That is something the present one hasn't done - as of this writing. And - if he can't prove it he deserves to be run out of Washington for lying to the American public and the World.

Sarah has shown that her ideas and beliefs are in line with the majority of citizens. She believes that the Tea Parties are a true representation of all God fearing and Country loving Americans. The Tea Party worked in 1773 and it's working in 2009/ 10.

Do not underestimate the power of Sarah Palin. She has sparked a fire that will turn into a blaze before 2012. Her 2008 Vice Presidential run was not a mistake as many in the Republican party claim. If she would have had more say in the campaign she might be in Washington today.

I'm sorry folks, but this is the turkey that was elected President

Ron Berger 15

PROUD MEMBER OF THE
Angry Mob
If you're not outraged, you're not paying attention.

FOR REAL CHANGE
VOTE OUT YOUR
CONGRESSMAN
IN 2010 !!!

I WANT YOU
to throw the bums out!

DIVERSITY
IT KILLED 13 AT FORT HOOD

Time for MORE TEA

Casa D'Ice
RESTAURANT & LOUNGE
CONGRESS & NANCY PELOSI
9 PERCENT APPROVAL RATING
THAT MEANS 91 PERCENT
SHOULD SHOULD SHOULD
HAVE NO PROBLEM
VOTING THEM OUT !!
www.casadice.com

Ron Berger 17

Thank you for reading this book. I know some won't like it, but then again, the truth hurts.

Please join me in the "Tea Party" that is going on as we speak. Nothing is more important than taking back the country that our founding fathers built and restoring our standing in the world.

www.teapartynation.com
www.teapartypatriots.com

Your participation is needed.

Thanks, Ron

May God Bless You All

Dear Ron,

"Thank you so much for sending me a copy of your book. You're a true patriot! Please continue to let your voice be heard. Todd and I were happy to receive your message and we appreciate your thoughtfulness for taking the time to write. . . "

Sarah Palin

Governor Palin was gracious enough to send me a thank you note for my first "Time for TEA" book. She will also get the first copy off the press with this one. I truly believe she is the best thing that has come out of the Republican Party since Ronald Reagan. To bring back some of the same old "hacks" will result in some of the same old "stuff".

Both parties have so much rotten baggage that only a new start will rectify this problem. When can you remember where both parties have had so many rotten apples in one barrel? Neither party is exempt from this problem. So many feel that they are special and deserve special treatment. However, they are to represent us and not pretend they are of a higher class. How can anyone believe that the law of the land was formulated by one party only while the other side totally vetoed it?

Maybe we need to change the way things are voted on.

I believe that the Republican party is still the best base to campaign on. More conservatives are aligned with Republicans than Democrats.

We are not looking for the same old crap that we have received over the last number of years. We are not looking for a Republican or Democrat to fill the vacancies we hope to generate in Washington this fall, but rather electing conservative over liberal will turn this country around. Do not be afraid to let your voice be heard. We need lots of voices to override the wrongs that are festering in our government.

I've left several pictures in from "Time for TEA" because I believe it shows the very soul of this man called Barrack Obama. I just can't imagine any American, let alone the President, giving the "crotch salute". The other picture also lets us know what he feels for his "subjects". I do not believe that middle finger was an accident but rather a true feeling of what he truly wishes for all of us.

All of us have noticed many other things that need to be accounted for. Here is just a sample:

**

This was written
by Sherry Hackett, Buddy Hackett's widow.

"WE NOTICED"
President Obama:

Today I read of your administrations' plan to re-define September 11 as a National Service Day. Sir, it's time we had a talk. During your campaign, Americans watched as you made mockery of our tradition of standing and crossing your heart when the Pledge of Allegiance was spoken. You, out of four people on the stage, were the only one not honoring our tradition.

YES, "We noticed."

During one of your many speeches, Americans heard you say that you intended to visit all 57 states.
We all know that Islam, not America has 57 states.

YES, "We noticed."

When President Bush leaned over at Ground Zero and gently placed a flower on the memorial, while you non-chalantly tossed your flower onto the pile without leaning over.

YES, "We noticed."

Every time you apologized to other countries for America 's position on an issue we have wondered why you don't share our pride in this great country.. When you have heard foreign leaders berate our country and our beliefs, you have not defended us. In fact, you insulted the British Crown beyond belief.

YES, "We noticed."

When your pastor of 20 years, "God-damned America " and said that 9/11 was " America 's chickens coming home to roost" and you denied having heard recriminations of that nature, we wondered how that could be. You later disassociated yourself from that church and Pastor Wright because it was politically expedient to do so.

YES, "We noticed."

When you announced that you would transform America , we wondered why. With all her faults, America is the greatest country on earth. Sir, KEEP THIS IN MIND, "if not for America and the people who built her, you wouldn't be sitting in the White House now." Prior to your election to the highest office in this Country, you were a senator from Illinois and from what we can glean from the records available, not a very remarkable one.

YES, "We noticed."

All through your campaign and even now, you have surrounded yourself with individuals who are basically unqualified for the positions for which you ap- pointed them. Worse than that, the majority of them are people who, like you, bear no special allegiance, respect, or affection for this country and her traditions.

YES, "We noticed."

You are 16 months into your term and every morning millions of Americans wake up to a new horror heaped on us by you. You seek to saddle working Americans with a health care/insurance reform package that, along with cap and trade, will bankrupt this nation.

YES, "We noticed."

We seek, by protesting, to let our representatives know that we are not in favor of these crippling expenditures and we are labeled "un-American","racist", "mob". We wonder how we are supposed   to let you know how frustrated we are. You have attempted to make our protests seem isolated and insignificant. Until your appointment, Americans had the right to speak out.

YES, "We noticed."

On September 11, 2001 there were no Republicans or Democrats, only Americans. And we all grieved together and helped each other in whatever way we could. The attack on 9/11 was carried out because we are Americans.

And YES, "We noticed."

There were many of us who prayed that as a black president you could help unite this nation. In six months you have done   more to destroy this nation than the attack on 9/11. You have failed us.

<u>YES, "We noticed."</u>

September 11 is a day of remembrance for all Americans. You propose to make 9/11 a "National Service Day". While we know that you don't share our reverence for 9/11, we pray that history will report your proposal as what it is, a disgrace.

<u>YES, "We noticed."</u>

You have made a mockery of our Constitution and the office that you hold. You have embarrassed and slighted us in foreign visits and policy.

<u>YES, "We noticed."</u>

We have noticed all these things. We will deal with you. When Americans come together again, it will be to remove you from office.

****

Not all criticism comes from within. The following is from Russia - yes Russia. They were our enemy for so many years and their newspaper, Pravda, was able to put their finger on what's wrong with the USA. Fellow Americans, please read the following slowly so that nothing is lost:

**

The following is an article that appeared in the national Russian newspaper Pravda recently. The authenticity of this piece was verified by Snopes link - http://www.snopes.com/politics/soapbo x/pravda.asp

<u>From Pravda a Russian Newspaper</u>
The irony of this article appearing in the English edition of Pravda (Russian on-line newspaper) defies description. Why can

a Russian newspaper print the following yet the American media can't/won't see it?

American Capitalism Gone With A Whimper

It must be said, that like the breaking of a great dam, the American descent into Marxism is happening with breath taking speed, against the back drop of a passive, hapless sheeple, excuse me dear reader, I meant people.

True, the situation has been well prepared on and off for the past century, especially the past twenty years. The initial testing grounds was conducted upon our Holy Russia and a bloody test it was. But we Russians would not just roll over and give up our freedoms and our souls, no matter how much money Wall

Street poured into the fists of the Marxists.

Those lessons were taken and used to properly prepare the American populace for the surrender of their freedoms and souls, to the whims of their elites and betters.

First, the population was dumbed down through a politicized and substandard education system based on pop culture, rather than the classics. Americans know more about their favorite TV dramas than the drama in DC that directly affects their lives. They care more for their "right" to choke down a McDonalds burger or a Burger King burger than for their constitutional rights. Then they turn around and lecture us about our rights and about our "democracy". Pride blinds the foolish.

Then their faith in God was destroyed, until their churches, all tens of thousands of different "branches and denominations" were for the most part little more than Sunday circuses and their televangelists and top protestant mega preachers were more than happy to sell out their souls and flocks to be on the "winning" side of one pseudo Marxist politician or another. Their flocks may complain, but when explained that they would be on the "winning" side, their flocks were ever so quick to reject Christ in hopes for earthly power. Even our Holy Orthodox churches are scandalously liberalized in America .

The final collapse has come with the election of Barack Obama. His speed in the past three months has been truly impressive. His spending and money printing has been a record setting, not just in America's short history but in the world. If this keeps up for more than another year, and there is no sign that it will not, America at best will resemble the Weimar Republic and at worst Zimbabwe.

These past two weeks have been the most breath taking of all. First came the announcement of a planned redesign of the American Byzantine tax system, by the very thieves who used it to bankroll their thefts, losses, and swindles of hundreds of billions of dollars. These make our Russian oligarchs look little more than ordinary street thugs, in comparison. Yes, the Americans have beat our own thieves in the shear volumes. Should we congratulate them?

These men, of course, are not an elected panel but made up of appointees picked from the very financial oligarchs and their henchmen who are now gorging themselves on trillions of American dollars, in one bailout after another. They are also usurping the rights, duties, and powers of the American congress (parliament). Again, congress has put up little more than a whimper to their masters.

Then came Barack Obama ' s command that GM ' s (General Motors) president step down from leadership of his company.   That is correct, dear reader, in the land of "pure" free markets, the American president now has the power, the self-given power, to fire CEOs and we can assume other employees of private companies, at will. Come hither, go dither, the centurion commands his minions.

So it should be no surprise, that the American president has followed this up with a "bold" move of declaring that he and another group of unelected, cho-sen stooges will now redesign the entire automotive industry and will even be the guarantee of automobile policies.. I am sure that if given the chance, they would happily try and redesign it for the whole of the world, too. Prime Minister Putin, less than two months ago, warned Obama and UK ' s Blair, not to follow the path to Marxism, it only leads to disaster. Apparently, even though we suffered 70 years of this Western sponsored horror show, we know nothing, as foolish, drunken Russians, so let our "wise" Anglo-Saxon fools find out the folly of their own pride.

Again, the American public has taken this with barely a whimper...but a "free man" whimper.

So, should it be any surprise to discover that the Democratically controlled Congress of America is working on passing a new regulation that would give the American Treasury department the power to set "fair" maximum salaries, evaluate performance, and control how private companies give out pay raises and bonuses? Senator Barney Frank, a social pervert basking in his homosexuality (of course, amongst the modern, enlightened American societal norm, as well as that of the general West, homosexuality is not only not a looked down upon life choice, but is often praised as a virtue) and his Marxist enlightenment, has led this effort. He stresses that this only affects companies that receive government monies, but it is retroactive and taken to a logical extreme, this would include any company or industry that has ever received a tax break or incentive.

The Russian owners of American companies and industries should look thoughtfully at this and the option of closing their facilities down and fleeing the land of the Red as fast as possible. In other words, divest while there is still value left.

The proud American will go down into his slavery without a fight, beating his chest, and proclaiming to the world, how free he really is. The world will only snicker.

****

Are you able to get your arms around this? Russia is telling us what our problems are? We, for years have been telling Russia how to live and now the tables are turned.

It doesn't take much to realize that what they are saying is true. B.O. has led us all down the wrong path. He said one thing in the campaign and does another now that he is in office.

His knowledge of finance is minimal and he picks out numbers to impress people but has no idea what they mean. He speaks of a million dollars like it was a big number. To you and I it is, but to B.O.'s budget it's nothing.

If he really wanted to save some money he should leave Air Force One on the ground more often instead of pretending it's just his personal taxi.

When he arrived in LA recently, the number of vehicles, planes, helicopters and personnel needed for his "fund raising trip" for Senator Boxer was frightening.   The trip could have never raised enough money to just pay his way to LA. What a waste. He thinks that now he is "king" of the USA he needs to take advantage of all the "perks" - all the time.

I think he feels that since his "forefathers" suffered so much that much is owed him and by golly he's going to take advantage of it. The country owes him all these perks.

One thing is for sure.   He doesn't know where he was born - or he doesn't want anyone to know. Why doesn't he prove - once and for all - he is a naturalized citizen of the USA?   The answer is simple - HE CAN'T!   Your President is a LIAR.

How come the "free press" hasn't delved into this problem? President Bush was raked over the coals about his military service to such an extent that you thought it would never end.   How dare the President claim that National Guard service has something to do with the military? Let's face it folks - It's a hell of lot more service in the military than our present occupier of the White House.

B.O. Is not experienced in anything. He only spent 143 days in the US Senate and was just a one term legislator in Illinois. He was a "rabble rouser" and enjoyed watching the flag burn and listen-

Ing to the Pastor Wright "God Damn America".

**

I THINK IT IS REMARKABLE THAT THE PRESS CAN FIND EVERY WOMAN WITH WHOM TIGER HAS HAD AN AFFAIR IN THE LAST FEW YEARS, WITH PHOTOS, TEXT MESSAGES, RECORDED PHONE CALLS, ETC. THEY KNOW NOT ONLY THE CAUSE OF THE FAMILY FIGHT, BUT THEY EVEN KNOW IT WAS A WEDGE FROM HIS GOLF BAG THAT SHE USED TO BREAK OUT THE WINDOWS IN THE ESCALADE. NOT ONLY THAT, THEY KNOW WHICH WEDGE!!!

THIS IS THE SAME PRESS (OR IS IT?) THAT CANNOT LOCATE OBAMA'S OFFICIAL BIRTH CERTIFICATE ... OR ANY OF HIS PAPERS WHILE IN COLLEGE......OR HOW HE PAID FOR A HARVARD EDUCATION...(or Michelle Obama's Princeton thesis on racism.) .... OR WHY BOTH HE AND MI-CHELLE VOLUNTEERED TO GIVE UP THEIR LAW DEGREES.

TRULY REMARKABLE!!!!!

****

Some very good questions. I would hope that the press would investigate and give us some answers. Here are some more questions:

**

The following is a narrative taken from a 2008 Sunday morning televised "Meet The Press'. The author (Dale Lindsborg) is employed by none other than the very liberal Washington Post!!

From Sunday's 07 Sept. 2008 11:48:04 EST, Televised "Meet the Press" THE THEN Senator Obama was asked about his stance on the American Flag.

General Bill Ginn' USAF (ret.) asked Obama to explain WHY he doesn't follow protocol when the National Anthem is played.

The General stated to Obama that according to the United States Code, Title 36, Chapter 10, Sec. 171...During rendition of the national anthem, when the flag is displayed, all present (except those in uniform) are expected to stand at attention facing the flag with the right hand over the heart. Or, at the very least, "Stand and Face It".

NOW GET THIS !! - - - - -

'Senator' Obama replied:

"<u>As I've said about the flag pin, I don't want to be perceived as taking sides</u>". "<u>There are a lot of people in the world to whom the American flag is a symbol of oppression..</u>" "<u>The anthem itself conveys a war-like message. You know, the bombs bursting in air and all that sort of thing.</u>"

(ARE YOU READY FOR THIS???)

Obama continued: "The National Anthem should be 'swapped' for something less parochial and less bellicose. I like the song 'I'd Like To Teach the World To Sing'. If that were our anthem, then, I might salute
it. In my opinion, we should consider re-inventing our National Anthem

as well as 'redesign' our Flag to better offer our enemies hope and love.

It's my intention, if elected, to disarm
America to the level of acceptance
to our Middle East Brethren. If we, as a
Nation of waring people, conduct ourselves like the nations of Islam, where
peace prevails - - - perhaps a
state or period of mutual accord could
exist between our governments ."

When I become President, I will seek a
pact of agreement to end hostilities between those who have been at war or in
a state of enmity, and a freedom from
disquieting oppressive thoughts. <u>We as a
Nation, have placed upon the nations
of Islam, an unfair injustice which is WHY
my wife disrespects the Flag and she
and I have attended several flag burn-
ing ceremonies in the past</u>".

"Of course now, I have found myself about to become the President of the United States and I have put my hatred aside. I will use my power to bring CHANGE to this Nation, and offer the people a new path..My wife and I look forward to becoming our Country's First black Family. <u>Indeed, CHANGE is about to overwhelm the United States of America</u> "

WHAAAAAAT, the Hell is that!!!

Yes, you read it right.

I, for one, am speechless!!!

Dale Lindsborg , Washington Post

****

He said his change would overwhelm the United States of America and over 50% of the voters bought into it. I believe now everyone is seeing what kind of change he meant and it certainly isn't the kind of change you voted for.

Whenever you hear someone say they disrespect something you can bet that their feelings don't leave them anytime soon. Neither Mrs. B.O. and B.O. himself have changed the color of their stripes. Just the way they act tells you that their feelings haven't changed and I'm sure they are laughing at how they pulled the wool over "whit-ties" eyes - as well as other races - and now just dare to get them out. You can't get them out - they're to big and you better not say anything bad about them or you will pay.   Their "hit list" is even longer than Nixon's.

Their ability to strike back is just like the Clinton's.   Those that disagree with them are racists, agitators, terrorists, right wingers, seditionists or what-ever.   And - if you are a Tea Party member, you must be totally misled.

The only person who is totally mis-led is the President himself.   Anytime you listen to a pastor, for over 20 years, who asks God to damn America you just know he is not fit to live here.   Then when the public calls him on it he reluctantly diminishes the relevance of Pastor's Wright's wranglings.   He eventually sepa-rates himself from Pastor Wright to keep the turmoil from getting out of control.

**

Sen. Barack Obama's pastor says blacks should not sing "God Bless America" but "God damn America."

Time for MORE TEA

The Rev. Jeremiah Wright has made a number of controversial statements.

The Rev. Jeremiah Wright, Obama's pastor for the last 20 years at the Trinity United Church of Christ on Chicago's south side, has a long history of what even Obama's campaign aides concede is "inflammatory rhetoric," including the assertion that the United States brought on the 9/11 attacks with its own "terrorism."

In a campaign appearance earlier this month, Sen. Obama said, "I don't think my church is actually particularly controversial." He said Rev. Wright "is like an old uncle who says things I don't always agree with," telling a Jewish group that everyone has someone like that in their family.

Rev. Wright married Obama and his wife Michelle, baptized their two daughters

Ron Berger   49

and is credited by Obama for the title of his book, "The Audacity of Hope."

TRINITY UNITED CHURCH OF CHRIST
REV DR JEREMIAH WRIGHT

****

Here are some more B.O. lies from his campaign. There just doesn't seem to be a shortage of these. I sure hope that those that voted for him realize how bad this election is for the country.

**

Mathew Staver, Founder and Chairman Liberty Counsel

You and I have just witnessed one of the most corrupt legislative sessions in American history. Now we have learned that one of the key "experts" pushing ObamaCare was also bought and paid for!

Please read below- Mat

The New York Times has exposed Jonathan Gruber, a professor of economics at M.I.T., as having published an article on their Op-Ed page supporting ObamaCare without disclosing that he had an ongoing consulting relationship with HHS. The Times noted that Professor Gruber had signed a contract obligating him to reveal such relationships. It would have been impossible for him to "forget" his consultancy - he had nearly $400,000 worth of lucrative contracts with HHS at the time!

++But wait - it gets much, much worse...

Popular blog site Firedoglake revealed last Friday that the Obama Administration has paid Gruber more than $780,000 in TAX DOLLARS to make the public case for health care reform! Jonathan Gruber's work has been extensively cited by the White House, Members of Congress, and the media continuously since ObamaCare came onto the scene, but NOT ONCE did anyone in the administration disclose he was on their payroll!

Here's Gruber's lame explanation: "All my editorials or public reports have been done on my own time." I guess he expects us to believe that his views weren't influenced by the nearly one million dollars he's gotten so far!

++More "Chicago on the Potomac"

The Jonathan Gruber revelation is just the latest public exposure of the graft and dishonesty which has characterized the way the Obama/Pelosi/Reid power axis has advanced ObamaCare. Given what we know, can you imagine what else is under the table?!

Just before Christmas, Senate Majority Leader Harry Reid sytematically bought off every Democrat member of the Senate who could possibly derail his crucial cloture vote. When all the "bribes" were handed out, Reid had the required 60 votes to choke off debate in the middle of the night. The congressional leadership and the Obama White House arm twisters have literally drug our nation down to the level of a cheap banana republic! They know their popular support is plummeting. They have become desperate and will stop at nothing.

Honest Americans have been nauseated as we have learned:

** Senator Mary Landrieu (D-LA) received $300 million in extra federal spending for her state in what critics derisively called "The Louisiana Purchase."

** Senator Ben Nelson (D-NE) accepted a deal exempting his state from new Medicaid costs and several other long-term perks. Nelson's purchase has been dubbed the "Cornhusker Kick Back."

** Many other bribes and "special provisions" affected the states of Vermont, North and South Dakota, Wyoming, Massachusetts, Hawaii, Michigan, Florida, and Connecticut.

But perhaps most painful of all, we have watched a smug Harry Reid justifying his corrupt acts by suggesting it is every senator's DUTY to get pay-offs for their votes! "If they don't have something in it important to them, then it doesn't speak well of them," Reid said in a post-cloture interview. So much for the integrity of the United States Senate!

++On top of all the corruption, ObamaCare is unconstitutional. If you wondered why Harry Reid rushed his 2,074-page bill and its 383-page "Manager's Amendment" through in the middle of the night with just hours to read them, then here's at least one answer...

Right there on page 1,020, the tyrannical Senate majority insists that no future Congress can repeal or otherwise amend the section on "Independent Medical Advisory Boards."

You will probably remember that socialists mocked Governor Sarah Palin for calling such independent boards "death panels." Yet Governor Palin was correct in her assessment - what else would you call boards with the power to grant or deny life-saving care using some pseudo-scientific "cost-benefit" formula?

Carefully hidden away in Reid's version of ObamaCare is a section that gives these boards far more power and permanence than the Constitution allows to ANY government entity!

++ If this bill becomes law, Liberty Counsel will challenge its constitutionality in court!

Every version of ObamaCare we've seen so far is unconstitutional because:

1) Congress has NO authority to force every American to carry insurance coverage, and,

2) Congress has NO authority to fine employers whose policies do not have the mandated coverage.

If this monstrous healthcare bill passes, it must be strongly challenged in the federal judiciary from the moment of its birth.   Liberty Counsel will do exactly that!

++But for now, especially since there is an increasing outcry

against ObamaCare's corruption, we MUST continue to make Congress hear our voice!

We are going all out to BURY Congress in protest over this endless procession of dirty tricks. And it looks like ObamaCare is more vulnerable than ever due to the recent sordid revelations of bribery and scandal.

Americans nationwide are expressing OUTRAGE at this overt manipulation and total lack of integrity. Reid, Pelosi and Obama have proven they will do any-thing to get this government takeover of our medical industry.

****

**

Barack Obama said, "To close that credibility gap we must take action on both ends of Pennsylvania Avenue to end the outsized influence of lobbyists; to do our work openly; and to give our people the government they deserve.

"That's what I came to Washington to do. That's why - for the first time in history - my Administration posts our White House visitors online. And that's why we've excluded lobbyists from policy-making jobs or seats on federal boards and commissions."

Maybe this explains why his national security policies are so weak. He put William Lynn in the Pentagon as Deputy Defense Secretary. Mr. Lynn was a lobbyist for Defense Contractor Ratheon. I guess the Deputy Defense Secretary is not a policy-making job.

<u>But it is not just Lynn.</u>

<u>Eric Holder</u>, attorney general nominee, was registered to lobby until 2004 on behalf of clients including Global Crossing, a bankrupt telecommunications firm [now confirmed].

<u>Tom Vilsack</u>, secretary of agriculture nominee, was registered to lobby as recently as last year on behalf of the National Education Association.

<u>William Lynn</u>, deputy defense secretary nominee, was registered to lobby as recently as last year for defense contractor Raytheon, where he was a top executive.

<u>William Corr</u>, deputy health and human services secretary nominee, was registered to lobby until last year for the Campaign for Tobacco-Free Kids, a nonprofit that pushes to limit tobacco use.

<u>David Hayes</u>, deputy interior secretary nominee, was registered to lobby until

2006 for clients, including the regional utility San Diego Gas & Electric.

Mark Patterson, chief of staff to Treasury Secretary Timothy Geithner, was registered to lobby as recently as last year for financial giant Goldman Sachs.

Ron Klain, chief of staff to Vice President Joe Biden, was registered to lobby until 2005 for clients, including the Coalition for Asbestos Resolution, U.S. Airways, Airborne Express and drug-maker ImClone.

Mona Sutphen, deputy White House chief of staff, was registered to lobby for clients, including Angliss International in 2003.

Melody Barnes, domestic policy council director, lobbied in 2003 and 2004 for liberal advocacy groups, including the American Civil Liberties Union, the Leadership Conference on Civil Rights, the American Constitution Society and the Center for Reproductive Rights.

Cecilia Munoz, White House director of intergovernmental affairs, was a lobbyist as recently as last year for the National Council of La Raza, a Hispanic advocacy group.

Patrick Gaspard, White House political affairs director, was a lobbyist for the Service Employees International Union.

Michael Strautmanis, chief of staff to the president's assistant for intergovernmental relations, lobbied for the American Association of Justice from 2001 until 2005.

Sincerely yours,

Erick Erickson
Editor, RedState.com

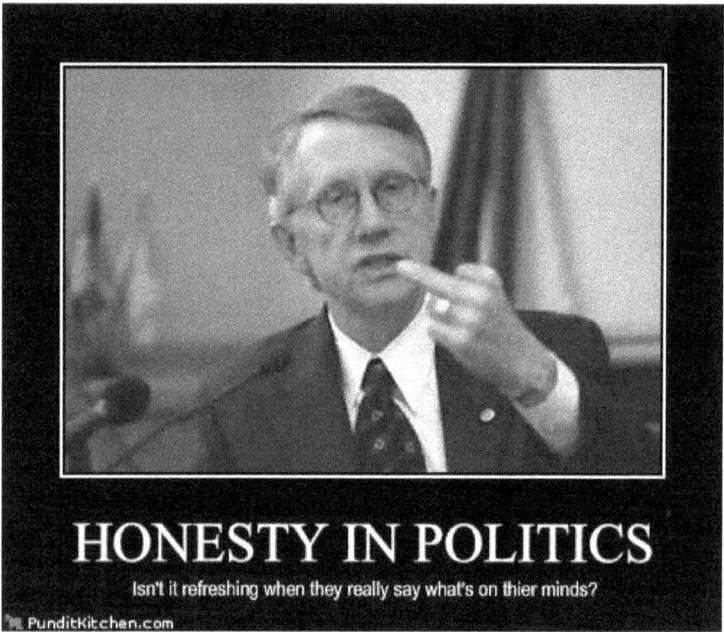

HONESTY IN POLITICS

Isn't it refreshing when they really say what's on thier minds?

PunditKitchen.com

Now you know what Sen. Reid thinks of YOU.

**

Obama "Consumer Protection Czar" Linked to Goldman Sachs Mortgage Scandal

Harry Reid has threatened to start forcing the Democratic financial overhaul bill through the Senate early next week. The bill would create yet another new bureaucracy, the "Consumer Financial Protection Agency" with the power to impose new government regulation on millions of financial transactions. President Obama's rumored pick to run the CFPA is a Treasury official with a disturbing history of ties to shady lending, bank bailouts, and massive donations from subprime mortgage billionaires.

Deputy Assistant Secretary Eric Stein is the former senior vice president of an activist and lobbying group called the Center for Responsible Lending (CRL). While Stein was running CRL in 2007, he received a $15 million donation from hedge fund manager John Paulson.

Paulson is notorious due to his central role in the SEC's case charging Goldman Sachs in a complex mortgage fraud scheme. In 2007, at the same time that Paulson was betting billions against the US housing market, his $15 million donation to CRL enabled the group to hire more lobbyists to push its radical agenda. Paulson took home $3.7 billion that year, even while hundreds of thousands of American homeowners lost their houses to foreclosure.

John Paulson isn't the only subprime magnate Eric Stein shares a special relationship with. CRL also received at least $15 million from Herb and Marion Sandler. The Sandlers pioneered so-called "Pick-a-Pay" mortgages, and made $2.4 billion when they sold their subprime lending business to Wachovia in 2007. Wachovia ended up losing billions of dollars on the sale, and the SEC and Justice Department have been investigating allegations that the Sandlers' company made fraudulent claims to investors. Time Magazine featured them in a story titled "25 People to Blame for the Financial Crisis."

During his tenure at CRL, Stein advocated for increased lending to borrowers with bad credit histories, and his "Self-Help" organization sold those mortgages on the secondary loan market. A primary purchaser of CRL-linked loans was Stein's previous employer, Fannie Mae, which has received at least $76 billion in taxpayer bailout funds.

Eric Stein has shown a disturbing willingness to do business with people who have devastated the nation's economy. Putting him in charge of the CFPA would give him tremendous power and control over a $400 million bureaucracy.

We need a real shepherd to watch the flock, not another Wall Street wolf in sheep's clothing.

****

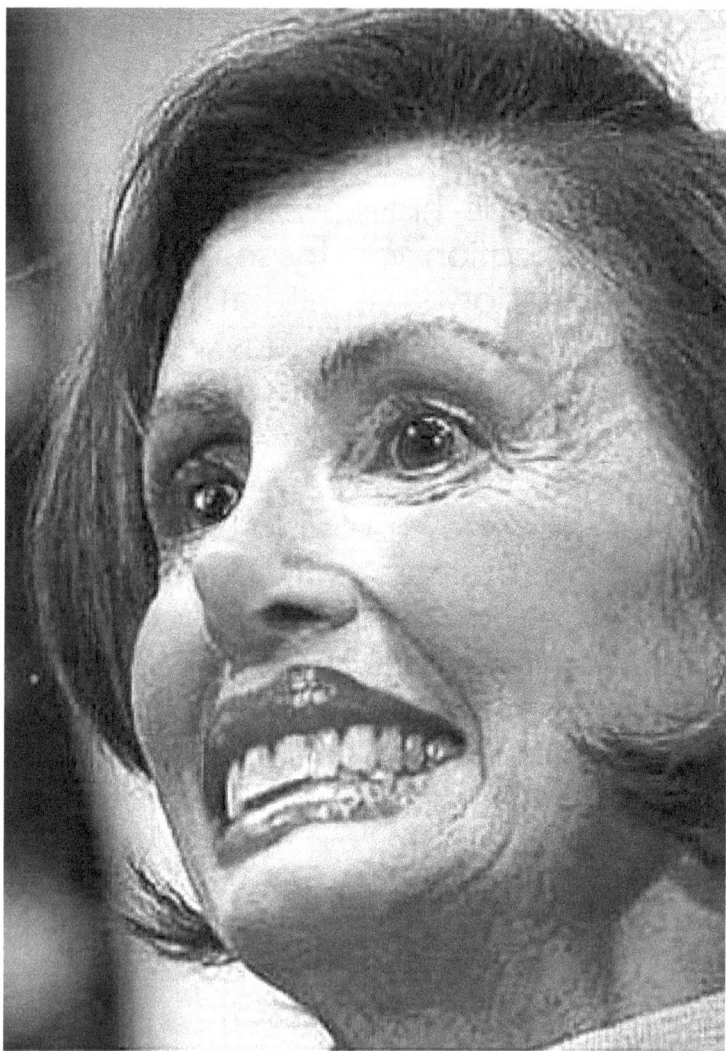

Now this is scary

GOT SOCIALISM?

The dynamic duo working for the Joker

Now if you think nothing new happens in Washington except the bad news - well here is an item hot off the press that I'm sure you will be excited to know.

**

311- A Dangerous New Element!

Discovery Announcement ~ The densest element in the known Universe has been found!

Pelosium: A major research institution has just announced the discovery of the densest element yet known to science. The new element has been named Pelosium. Pelosium has one neutron, 12 assistant neutrons, 75 deputy neutrons, and 223 assistant deputy neutrons, giving it an atomic mass of 311.

These particles are held together by dark forces called morons, which are surrounded by vast quantities of lepton-like particles called peons. The symbol of Pelosium is PU.

Pelosium's mass actually increases over time, as morons randomly interact with various elements in the atmosphere and become assistant deputy neutrons within the Pelosium molecule, leading to the formation of isodopes.

This characteristic of moron-promotion leads some scientists to believe that Pe-

Iosium is formed whenever morons reach a certain quantity in concentration.

****

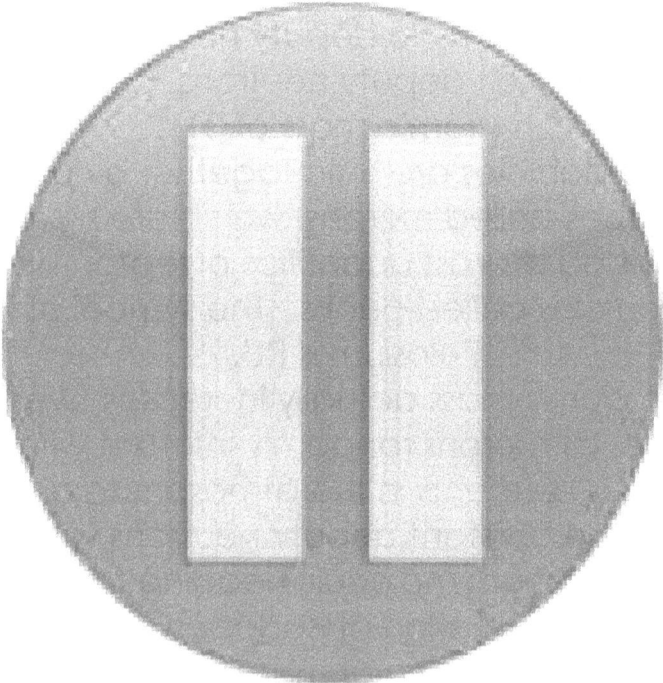

I've had to pause here for awhile. I get so rapped up in how the present government is behaving that I have trouble keeping a civil tongue in my mouth. I'm sure you don't want to hear all the words I have not written here.

Besides, this gives me a little time to mull over the next part of the book and try and present it in a civilized fashion without an "R" rating.

The pause time varies from book to book. One book took a pause time of several years and another may only require several weeks.

I'm sure you can relate to being blasted with "stupidity" everyday for weeks on end and having your mind grow numb. It's like they say - "the only way to get rid of stupidity is to vote it out."

We are afforded a precious element this year (2010) to vote out all incumbents and start fresh with "freshmen" in the House and one third "newbies" in the Senate. That would be enough to turn this country around and start fresh. If we don't, this fiasco will continue for at least another two years.

This is NOT heated rhetoric from the evil "right" or slanderous mouthings from possible terrorists, but FACTS from America's faithful.

When the country starts to go downhill it is not noticed for a long time. We, as Americans, tend to allow extra time and do a lot of forgiving to grant the government time to get things right. However, it's very much like a car tire that has a slow leak and is not noticed until it is totally flat. The damage then has been done and it is costly to repair. WAKE UP AMERICA - our tire is going flat!

Thank you for allowing me this break. I hope that the rest of the book can be read in public.

Ron

FORWARD

I may pause for a few days more so I can recover from a case of the "H1S1" flu. (The House & Senate flu that's going around) This stuff really makes you sick - doesn't it?

Ron Berger   73

It's ironic that for eight years of the Bush administration the Democrats blasted him for how much money was spent and why we got into the wars in Iraq and Afghanistan. Now that "change " has been made the Demo-crats have doubled the deficit and are about to lose the war in Afghanistan.

Yes - we are at war with Islam and if we don't defeat them we will forever be sorry. Their only aim in life is to extermi-nate the infidels. The word infidel refers to non-islam believers. That pretty much takes in everyone left on the planet.

B.O. has stated that if push comes to shove he will be on the Islam side. He has disavowed his mother for being white and given all his up bringing credit to his African born father.

He has also disavowed the feeling that the American flag is a symbol of pa-triotism and the anthem is the sound of freedom. He has inserted Islam into the history of the United States of America where there is no place. He has taken out God as the anchor of our nation and substituted Muhammad as the Savior to pray to. This is our Commander-in-Chief that refuses to honor and salute the flag. This is the person who is in charge of guiding our country to peace and prosperity and neither has come close to reality. We are about to go into a prolonged inflation cycle that will be just as bad as the recession cycle we are just coming out of.

Like the story goes - B.O. Hasn't even run a Dairy Queen and now he's in charge of the nation's finances. Lord Have Mercy!

Please don't give me that line that Islam is the "radical" arm of the Muslim religion and all the "regular" Muslims just want to live in peace. They all read the same Quran and that teaches what they are to do with their lives. Read the book - "The Truth about Muhammad" by Robert Spencer. I'm not making this up folks. The Quran states that <u>all infidels are to be killed wherever they are found.</u>

**

Barack OBAMA, in his Cairo speech, said: "I know, too, that Islam has always been a part of America 's story."

AN AMERICAN CITIZEN'S RESPONSE:

Dear Mr. Obama:

Were those Muslims that were in America when the Pilgrims first landed? Funny, I thought they were Native American Indians.

Were those Muslims that celebrated the first Thanksgiving day? Sorry again, those were Pilgrims and Native American Indians.

Can you show me one Muslim signature on the United States Constitution?

Declaration of Independence ?

Bill of Rights?

Didn't think so.

Did Muslims fight for this country's freedom from England ? No.

Did Muslims fight during the Civil War to free the slaves in America ? No, they did not. In fact, Muslims to this day are still the largest traffickers in human slavery. Your own half brother, a devout Muslim, still advocates slavery himself, even though Muslims of Arabic descent refer to black Muslims as "pug nosed slaves." Says a lot of what the Muslim world really thinks of your family's "rich Islamic heritage," doesn't it Mr. Obama?

Where were Muslims during the Civil Rights era of this country? Not present.

There are no pictures or media accounts of Muslims walking side by side with Martin Luther King, Jr. or helping to advance the cause of Civil Rights.

Where were Muslims during this country's Woman's Suffrage era? Again, not present. In fact, devout Muslims demand that women are subservient to men in the Islamic culture. So much so, that often they are beaten for not wearing the 'hajib' or for talking to a man who is not a direct family member or their husband. Yep, the Muslims are all for women's rights, aren't they?

Where were Muslims during World War II? They were aligned with Adolf Hitler. The Muslim grand mufti himself met with Adolf Hitler, reviewed the troops and accepted support from the Nazi's in killing Jews.

Finally, Mr. Obama, where were Muslims on Sept. 11th, 2001? If they weren't flying planes into the World Trade Center , the Pentagon or a field in Pennsylvania killing nearly 3,000 people on our own soil, they were rejoicing in the Middle East . No one can dispute the pictures shown from all parts of the Muslim world celebrating on CNN, Fox News, MSNBC and other cable news networks that day. Strangely, the very "moderate" Muslims whose rears you bent over backwards to kiss in Cairo , Egypt on June 4th were stone cold silent post 9-11. To many Americans, their silence has meant approval for the acts of that day.

And THAT, Mr. Obama, is the "rich heritage" Muslims have here in America .

Oh, I'm sorry, I forgot to mention the Barbary Pirates. They were Muslim.

And now we can add November 5, 2009 - the slaughter of American soldiers at Fort Hood by a Muslim major who is a doctor and a psychiatrist who was supposed to be counseling soldiers returning from battle in Iraq and Afghanistan .

That, Mr. Obama is the "Muslim heritage" in America .

****

And now words of wisdom from his books that made him so much money last year. Words spoken like a "true American".

**

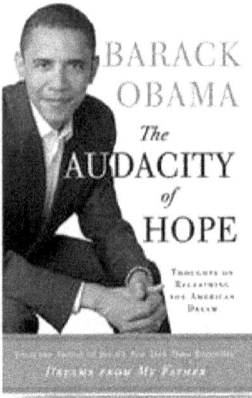

THIS IS OUR PRESIDENT –
Is anyone out there awake?

Everyone of voting age should read
these two books: Don't buy them, just
get them from the library.

From Dreams of My Father: "I ceased to
advertise my mother's race at the age of
12 or 13, when I began to suspect that
by doing so I was ingratiating myself to
whites."

From Dreams of My Father : "I found a solace in nursing a pervasive sense of grievance and animosity against my mother's race."

From Dreams of My Father: "There was something about her that made me wary, a little too sure of herself, maybe and white."

From Dreams of My Father: "It remained necessary to prove which side you were on, to show your loyalty to the black masses, to strike out and name names."

From Dreams of My Father: "I never emulate white men and brown men whose fates didn't speak to my own. It was into my father's image, the black man, son of Africa, that I'd packed all the attributes I sought in myself: the attributes of Martin and Malcolm, DuBois and Mandela."

And FINALLY ....
and most scary:

From Audacity of Hope:
"I will stand with the Muslims should the political winds shift in an ugly direction."

****

Can anything be more scary? Fellow Americans, we are knee deep in sheep dip and it's really starting to stink! Our president refuses to show his birth certificate and his class records which indicates that he is hiding information that, we the public, have a right to know. Here's what some of his "classmates" have to say:

**

WHO the HELL IS HE ???

IS THIS TRUE?????

Read this....

I did some of my own research after reading this. Why was his law license inactivated in 2002?

Why was Michelle's law license INACTIVATED by court order?

There is only one Barack Hussein Obama according to the U. S. Census and he has 27 Social Security numbers and over 80 aliases.

The one he uses now originated in Connecticut where he is not ever reported to have lived.   No wonder ALL of his 'records' are sealed!!!

It just gets worse!!!

At least we only have 3 years of this mystery man left before we can replace him.

Was He There?

Who IS He?

I have always wondered why NO ONE ever came forward from Obama's past saying they knew him, attended school with him, was his friend, etc.

NO ONE, not one person has ever come forward from his past.

VERY, VERY STRANGE.

This should really be a cause for great concern.

To those who voted for him, YOU HAVE ELECTED THE BIGGEST UNQUALIFIED FRAUD that America has ever known!

This is very interesting stuff. Sort of adds credence to the idea of The Manchurian Candidate thing having happened here!

Stephanopoulos of ABC news said the same thing during the 08' campaign. He too was a classmate of BO's at Columbia class of 1984. He said he never had ONE class with him.

Was he there?

While he is such a great orator, why doesn't ANYONE in Obama's college class remember him?

Maybe he never attended class!

Maybe he never attended Columbia?

He won't allow Colombia to release his records either.

Suspicious isn't it???

NOBODY REMEMBERS OBAMA AT CO-LUMBIA!!!!!!!

Looking for evidence of Obama's past, Fox News contacted 400 Columbia University students from the period when Obama claims to have been there, but none remembered him.

Wayne Allyn Root was, like Obama, a political science major at Columbia who also graduated in 1983.

In 2008, Root says of Obama, "I don't know a SINGLE PERSON at Columbia that knew him, and they all know me.

I don't have a classmate who ever knew Barack Obama at Columbia.   EVER! Nobody recalls him.

I'm not exaggerating, I'm not kidding.

"Root adds that he was also, like Obama, "Class of '83 political science, pre-law" and says, "You don't get more exact or closer than that.

Never met him in my life, don't know anyone who ever met him.

At the class reunion, our 20th reunion five years ago, who was asked to be the speaker of the class?   Me. No one ever heard of Barack!

And five years ago, nobody even knew who he was.   The guy who writes the class notes, who's kind of the, as we say in New York, the macha who knows everybody, has yet to find a person, a human who ever met him.

Is that not strange?   It's VERY strange. "Obama's photograph does NOT appear in the school's 'yearbook' and Obama consistently declines requests to talk about his years at Columbia, provide school records, or provide the name of any former classmates or friends while at Columbia.
http://en.wikipedia.org/wiki/Wayne_Allyn_Root#column-one

NOTE: Root graduated as Valedictorian from his high school, Thornton-Donovan School, then graduated from Columbia University in 1983 as a Political Science major (in the same class as Barack Hussein Obama WAS SUPPOSED TO HAVE BEEN IN).

Can it be that BHO is a complete fraud??

More intrigue concerning "The Man who WASN'T there."

****

**

As a reminder, Time Square a few weeks ago !!!!!!

Following is an email we received from a former Muslim. We are reprinting it with his permission:

I was born and raised as Muslim. My name is Abdul Rahman. My whole family is still Muslim. I know the Islamic brain very well. I have lived and breathed with them. I am an insider. I left Islam when I understood Islam is a sick and evil religion. Muslims can fool the gullible West but can't fool us, the ex-Muslims. On this basis I write the following:

Fighting terrorism is easier than fighting the evil teachings of Islam. These evil teachings are already inside the West.

Muslims do not need Osama Bin Laden or Zarqawi to lead them. Their inspiration for violence comes directly from the Quran and from Islamic history. One small independent group of Muslims in the West can create havoc.

Ali Sina, of FaithFreedom.org <http://www.news.faithfreedom.org/> , thinks he can bring down this 1400 years old religion in his lifetime. Is he dreaming? How can you defeat an enemy who has the following agenda? Also remember that the greatest strength of Muslims is that they do not read any site or books that talk against Islam. Most Muslims do not even read the Quran in their own language.

Who will tell you the truth about Islam? Muslims? Of course not. Muslims can't even see the evil in Islam. The West? The gullible West has no clue. Then who? Ex-Muslims and ex-Muslims only can expose Islam to the West. Muslims believe Islam will rule the world, very soon. They are committed to it. The constitution for the new Islamic Republic of EU and USA is under construction. Welcome to the 21st Century Islamic Warfare. To the infidels of the West, Muslims say: We will fight the infidel to death. And they mean it. Meanwhile, Muslims are able to say with complete confidence:

American laws will protect us.
Democrats and Leftist will support us.
The UNO will legitimize us.
CAIR and MAB will incubate us.
The ACLU will support us.
Western Universities will educate us.
Mosques in the West will shelter us.
OPEC will finance us.
Moderate Muslims will fertilize us.
Hollywood will love us.
Koffi Annan will publish the politically correct sympathetic statements for Jihadists.
We will use your (West) welfare system.
We will take advantage of American kindness, gullibility, and compassion. When time comes, we will stab America in the back as we did on 9/11 and 7/7, the Islamic way. We will say one thing on the camera (Islam is the religion of

peace) and teach another thing (Quran 8:12 Terrorize and behead the infidels wherever you find them) to our children at home.

We will teach our children Islamic supremacy from their earliest childhood. We will take over Europe first and then the U.S. will be the next. We already have a solid ground in the UK, Holland, Sweden, Spain, Italy, Germany, and now in the U.S.

Who are we? We are the ³sleeper cells² next door.

At the time of the real fight we will hold our own children as our armor - this is the Islamic way. When American or Israeli troops shoot at us the world will be watching. Imagine, just imagine the news in the world: ³Death of Muslim babies by infidels².

We say to the West: Keep your Nukes in your curio cabinets. Keep your aircraft carriers and high-tech weaponry in the showcase. You can't use them against us because of your own higher moral standard. We will take the advantage of your (Western) higher moral standard and use it against you. We won't hesitate to use our children as suicide bombers against you.

The West manufactures their tanks in the factory. We Muslims will manufacture our military force by natural means (by producing more babies. It is cheaper that way. You infidels cannot defeat us. We are 1.2 billion strong and we will double our population again.

Using the Western legal system we will assert our Sharia <http://www.cfr.org/publication/8034/> Laws, slowly but surely.

Moderate Muslims will say there is no link between Islam and terrorism and the West will believe it because the West is so gullible. Moderate Muslims all over the world will inadvertently incubate Jihadists by defending Islam as a religion of peace, by telling this to their children and the world.

There will be more 9/11s in Europe and in America. We will say, [3]We do not support terrorism but America got what it deserved.[2]

We will recite the Quran and say Allah-Hu-Akbar before beheading infidels, as we have been doing it. We will video-tape those and send them to infidels to watch. The infidels will surrender (ISLAM means surrender.

Islam is the fastest growing religion among convicts in prison all over the word. 30% of French   prison inmates are already converted to Islam.

We will use your (Western) own values of kindness against you. You (the West) are destined to lose.

Must be very depressing for you (the West). Isn¹t it?

Allah-Hu-Akbar (as we like to say just before beheading you; it means God is Great).

The rules of war and intelligence-gathering that the world has evolved over the last 100 years count on some fundamental laws of humanity. For example there is some Geneva conventions even for the battlefield. For example, even in the battlefield you give enemy a chance to surrender. You do not take random hostages, behead them, videorecord it, and post it on the internet. Generally, a mother will try to save her babies and children (they won't sacrifice her own babies for her religion. These are basics of morality for the human race and have been for a very long time, even before religions came along.

Modern Islamic warfare did away with all of the above morality. The equation of war has changed. One major mistake the West has made is to believe terrorists need a structural hiarchical power structure to fight an enemy. Islamic teachings prepare Muslims from childhood to act on their own wherever they can (even without the authorization from his/her superiors. No wonder you are seeing so many independent Muslim terrorists all over the world. These are entrepreneur terrorists.

These sleeper cells go beyond national origin, language, race, or citizenship. Terrorists could be British born-and-raised citizens, or American Taliban. There is

only one thread that binds them together that is "ISLAM."

My, our (ex-Muslims'), message to the
West is until the West identifies, names,
and warns the public who the real enemy is, the West won't have chance to
win this war. The real enemy is "Islam." As
long as the world leaders are afraid to
call a spade a spade, and as long as
they keep saying in public the blatant lie
that ³Islam is a religion of peace² (we run
the risk losing our freedom.

Our freedom already is curtailed. No major newspapers, magazines, or TV repro-
duced the Mohammad cartoons in
America. They were afraid. So, in effect,
6 million Muslims in America and 1.2 billion Muslims around the globe severely
restricted our freedom of expression
without officially legislating their Sharia
laws that prohibits Mohammad's carica-
ture. We now have unwritten partial
Sharia laws in practice in the USA.

Remember ex-Muslims like me are the insiders. We are exposing Islam to the West so we can enjoy Western freedom. Our websites are: FaithFreedom.org <http://www.news.faithfreedom.org/> , and ApostatesOfIslam.com <http://apostatesofislam.com/> .

Qur'an 8:67 [3] It is not fitting for any prophet to have prisoners until he has made a great slaughter in the land.[2]

Qur'an 8:12 [3]I shall terrorize the infidels. So wound their bodies and incapacitate them because they oppose Allah and His Apostle.[2]
The author of the above is Abdul Rahman, who goes by an alias to protect himself from Islamic extremists. The Quran is very explicit in its treatment of apostates (people who leave the Muslim faith). The penalty for leaving Islam is death. Once you're in, you're in for good. Read what other apostates have written: <http://citizenwarrior2.blogspot.com/200

7/07/apostates-leaving-islam.html>.
Read more: The Terrifying Brilliance of the Islamic Memeplex
<http://citizenwarrior2.blogspot.com/200 7/10/terrifying-brilliance-of-islamic.html>
Read still more: The Life Of Muhammad
<http://www.thereligionofpeace.com/P ages/History.htm>

****

I can't tell you how scary this is. Please read this email again and let it sink in. This is worse than WW II. We were fighting nations that were, some-what, civilized in nature. They had the desire to rule the world and would have destroyed everything if we would have let them. Another email describes just how Germany made their presence known and how easy it was to over-come "sleeping nations".

**

The author of this article lives in South Dakota and appears to be very active in attempting to maintain our freedom. I encourage everybody to read this article and pass it along. I see so many parallels in this country–are we going to sit by and watch it happen? Spread the word; also contact your congressional reps; vote them out if they don't do what they should. If you don't want to be bothered, then you're part of the problem! Google Kitty Werthmann and you will see articles and videos.

Ron Berger   98

This truly is the Greatest Country in the World. Don't Let Freedom Slip Away

By: Kitty Werthmann

What I am about to tell you is something you've probably never heard or will ever read in history books.

I believe that I am an eyewitness to history. I cannot tell you that Hitler took Austria by tanks and guns; it would distort history. We elected him by a landslide - 98% of the vote.. I've never read that in any American publications.

Everyone thinks that Hitler just rolled in with his tanks and took Austria by force.

In 1938, Austria was in deep Depression. Nearly one-third of our workforce was unemployed.. We had 25% inflation and 25% bank loan interest rates.

Farmers and business people were declaring bankruptcy daily. Young people were going from house to house begging for food. Not that they didn't want to work; there simply weren't any jobs. My mother was a Christian woman and believed in helping people in need. Every day we cooked a big kettle of soup and baked bread to feed those poor, hungry people - about 30 daily.

The Communist Party and the National Socialist Party were fighting each other. Blocks and blocks of cities like Vienna , Linz , and Graz were destroyed.   The people became desperate and petitioned the government to let them decide what kind of government they wanted.
We looked to our neighbor on the north, Germany , where Hitler had been
in power since 1933. We had been told that they didn't have unemployment or crime, and they had a high standard of living. Nothing was ever said about persecution of any group -- Jewish or otherwise. We were led to believe that

everyone was happy. We wanted the same way of life in Austria . We were promised that a vote for Hitler would mean the end of unemployment and help for the family. Hitler also said that businesses would be assisted, and farmers would get their farms back. Ninety-eight percent of the population voted to annex Austria to Germany and have Hitler for our ruler.

We were overjoyed, and for three days we danced in the streets and had candlelight parades. The new government opened up big field kitchens and everyone was fed.

After the election, German officials were appointed, and like a miracle, we suddenly had law and order. Three or four weeks later, everyone was employed. The government made sure that a lot of work was created through the Public Work Service.

Hitler decided we should have equal rights for women. Before this, it was a custom that married Austrian women did not work outside the home. An able-bodied husband would be looked down on if he couldn't support his family. Many women in the teaching profession were elated that they could retain the jobs they previously had been required to give up for marriage.

Hitler targets Education - Eliminates Religious Instruction for Children:

Our education was nationalized. I attended a very good public school.. The population was predominantly Catholic, so we had religion in our schools. The day we elected Hitler (March 13, 1938), I walked into my schoolroom to find the crucifix replaced by Hitler's picture hanging next to a Nazi flag. Our teacher, a very devout woman, stood up and told the class we wouldn't pray or have religion anymore. Instead, we sang "Deutschland, Deutschland, Uber Alles," and had physical education.

Sunday became National Youth Day with compulsory attendance. Parents were not pleased about the sudden change in curriculum. They were told that if they did not send us, they would receive a stiff letter of warning the first time. The second time they would be fined the equivalent of $300, and the third time they would be subject to jail. The first two hours consisted of political indoctrination. The rest of the day we had sports.

As time went along, we loved it. Oh, we had so much fun and got our sports equipment free. We would go home and gleefully tell our parents about the wonderful time we had.

My mother was very unhappy. When the next term started, she took me out of public school and put me in a convent. I told her she couldn't do that and she told me that someday when I grew up, I would be grateful. There was a very good curriculum, but hardly any fun - no sports, and no political indoctrination. I hated it at first but felt I could tolerate it. Every once in a while, on holidays, I went home. I would go back to my old friends and ask what was going on and what they were doing. Their loose lifestyle was very alarming to me. They lived without religion. By that time unwed mothers were glorified for having a baby for Hitler. It seemed strange to me that our society changed so suddenly. As time went along, I realized what a great deed my mother did so that I wasn't exposed to that kind of humanistic philosophy.

Equal Rights Hits Home:
In 1939, the war started and a food bank was established. All food was rationed and could only be purchased using food stamps. At the same time, a full-employment law was passed which meant if you didn't work, you didn't get a ration card, and if you didn't have a card, you starved to death. Women who stayed home to raise their families didn't have any marketable skills and often had to take jobs more suited for men.

Soon after this, the draft was implemented. It was compulsory for young people, male and female, to give one year to the labor corps. During the day, the girls worked on the farms, and at night they returned to their barracks for military training just like the boys. They were trained to be anti-aircraft gunners and participated in the signal corps. After the labor corps, they were not discharged but were used in the front lines. When I go back to Austria to visit my family and friends, most of these women are emotional cripples because they just were not equipped to handle the horrors of combat.

Three months before I turned 18, I was severely injured in an air raid attack. I nearly had a leg amputated, so I was spared having to go into the labor corps and into military service.

Hitler restructured the Family Through Daycare:

When the mothers had to go out into the work force, the government immediately established child care centers. You could take your children ages 4 weeks to school age and leave them there around-the-clock, 7 days a week, under the total care of the government. The state raised a whole generation of children. There were no motherly women to take care of the children, just people highly trained in child psychology. By this time, no one talked about equal rights. We knew we had been had.

Health Care and Small Business
Suffer Under Government
Controls:

Before Hitler, we had very good medical care. Many American doctors trained at the University of Vienna . After Hitler, health care was socialized, free for everyone. Doctors were salaried by the government. The problem was, since it was free, the people were going to the doctors for everything. When the good doctor arrived at his office at 8 a.m., 40 people were already waiting and, at the same time, the hospitals were full. If you needed elective surgery, you had to wait a year or two for your turn. There was no money for research as it was poured into socialized medicine. Research at the medical schools literally stopped, so the best doctors left Austria and emigrated to other countries.

As for healthcare, our tax rates went up to 80% of our income. Newlyweds immediately received a $1,000 loan from the government to establish a household. We had big programs for families. All day care and education were free. High schools were taken over by the government and college tuition was subsidized. Everyone was entitled to free handouts, such as food stamps, clothing, and housing.

We had another agency designed to monitor business. My brother-in-law owned a restaurant that had square tables. Government officials told him he had to replace them with round tables

because people might bump themselves on the corners. Then they said he
had to have additional bathroom facilities. It was just a small dairy business with
a snack bar. He couldn't meet all the
demands.   Soon, he went out of
business. If the government owned the
large businesses and not many small
ones existed, it could be in control.

We had consumer protection. We were
told how to shop and what to buy. Free
enterprise was essentially abolished. We
had a planning agency specially designed for farmers. The agents would go
to the farms, count the live-stock, then
tell the farmers what to produce, and
how to produce it.
"Mercy Killing" Redefined:

In 1944, I was a student teacher in a
small village in the Alps.   The villagers
were surrounded by mountain passes
which, in the winter, were closed off with
snow, causing people to be isolated. So
people intermarried and offspring were
sometimes retarded.   When I arrived, I

was told there were 15 mentally retarded adults, but they were all useful
and did good manual work. I knew one,
named Vincent, very well. He was a
janitor of the school. One day I looked
out the window and saw Vincent and
others getting into a van. I asked my su-
perior where they were going. She said
to an institution where the State Health
Department would teach them a trade,
and to read and write. The families were
required to sign papers with a little
clause that they could not visit for 6
months. They were told visits would inter-
fere with the program and might cause
homesickness.

As time passed, letters started to dribble
back saying these people died a natural, merciful death. The villagers were
not fooled. We suspected what was
happening. Those people left in excel-
lent physical health and all died within 6
months. We called this euthanasia.

The
Final Steps - Gun Laws:

Next came gun registration. People were getting injured by guns. Hitler said that the real way to catch criminals (we still had a few) was by matching serial numbers on guns. Most citizens were law abiding and dutifully marched to the police station to register their firearms. Not long after-wards, the police said that it was best for everyone to turn in their guns. The authorities already knew who had them, so it was futile not to comply voluntarily.

No more freedom of speech. Anyone who said something against the government was taken away. We knew many people who were arrested, not only Jews, but also priests and ministers who spoke up.

Totalitarianism didn't come quickly, it took 5 years from 1938 until 1943, to realize full dictatorship in Austria . Had it happened overnight, my countrymen would have fought to the last breath. Instead, we had creeping gradualism.

Now, our only weapons were broom handles. The whole idea sounds almost unbelievable that the state, little by little eroded our freedom.

After World War II, Russian troops occupied Austria . Women were raped, preteen to elderly. The press never wrote about this either. When the Soviets left in 1955, they took everything that they could, dismantling whole factories in the process. They sawed down whole orchards of fruit, and what they couldn't destroy, they burned. We called it The Burned Earth. Most of the population barricaded themselves in their houses. Women hid in their cellars for 6 weeks as the troops mobilized. Those who couldn't, paid the price. There is a monument in Vienna today, dedicated to those women who were massacred by the Russians. This is an eye witness account.

"It's true..those of us who sailed past the Statue of Liberty came to a country of unbelievable freedom and opportunity.

America Truly is the Greatest Country in theWorld. Don't Let Freedom Slip Away,

"After America , There is No Place to Go"

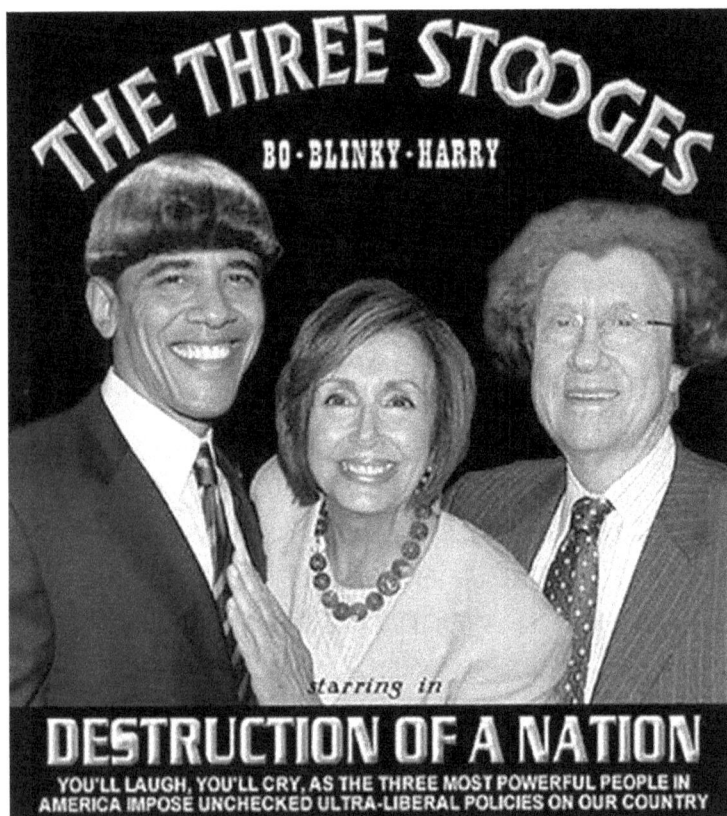

****

On a personal note - while at the mail box the other day, a neighbor, who just returned home after a long trip, asked why I hadn't sent him any emails recently. My answer was that I didn't want to bother him while he was enjoying his trip.

He let me know that everywhere they went they heard the same thing. Those that voted for B.O. didn't understand why they did and those that didn't still couldn't fathom why the others did. I received an email that I thought you might take to heart:

**

The danger to America is not Barack Obama but a citizenry capable of entrusting a man like him with the presidency. It will be easier to limit and undo the follies of an Obama presidency than to restore the necessary common sense and good judgment to an electorate willing to have such a man for their president. The problem is much deeper and far more serious than Mr. Obama, who is a mere symptom of what ails us. Blaming the prince of the fools should not blind anyone to the vast confederacy of fools that made him their prince. The republic can survive a Barack Obama. It is less likely to survive a multitude of fools such as those who made him their president.

-- Author Unknown

****

I leave you with this prayer written by a good friend from long ago. The prayer is new, but I've known her for over 50 years and her heart is right with GOD.

If you haven't done it before my friends, now is the time to bend those knees and call upon God to help.

HEAR OUR PRAYER OH GOD

Oh God I bow my heart and soul
I ask of you today
To humble all your children
As we kneel down to pray.
Our nation has been blinded
By Satan's awful lies
Now we lay in ruins
With our leader's alibis.

Forgive us for complacency
And our neglect to see
How our Godly nation
Has gone downhill so gradually.

We have lost your blessing
On this our native land
For we have sinned and left you out
Now helpless we do stand.

This our cry to heal our land
As we kneel down today.
We ask you for forgiveness
Please hear us as we pray.

Barbara Cook

Thank you Barbara, for that wonderful prayer. I just can't emphasize enough to all my readers how important prayer is. We have turned our backs on God for a long time and with the help of agencies like the ACLU we will completely erase God's name on everything important. We can't let that happen. We must beg for His forgiveness and ask that He help us turn things around and bring Him back to the center our our universe. God is the only One that can give us the strength to accomplish this and all we have to do is pray and ask for forgiveness.

"IF MY PEOPLE, WHICH ARE CALLED BY MY NAME, SHALL HUMBLE THEMSELVES AND PRAY AND SEEK MY FACE AND TURN FROM THEIR WICKED WAYS; THEN WILL I HEAR FROM HEAVEN AND WILL FORGIVE THEIR SIN AND WILL HEAL THEIR LAND,"
2 CHRONICLES 7:14

MAY GOD BLESS US ALL

End Note from the Author

I've made my books on Tea relatively short so that the "word" gets to be read quicker and more action can be taken. This is my second "Tea book" and I already have a feeling that a third is on the way.

The amount of information I am getting from various sources is overwhelming and I feel it packs a bigger wallop when put in a book. You cannot possibly ignore all this information. You know it's true, even if you are a B.O. supporter.

I've had a "fall-out" with my ex. pastor over this issue. He is so liberal that common sense just doesn't make sense to him. He knows the Bible, but can't see that B.O. Is leading the country down the wrong path of Islam.

Ron

www.ingramcontent.com/pod-product-compliance
Lightning Source LLC
Chambersburg PA
CBHW050534280326
41933CB00011B/1578